What Can Be Done?

**Indigenous Bi-Vocational Ministry
And Ministry Education By Extension**

By Vernon Swenson

Fairway Press
Lima, Ohio

WHAT CAN BE DONE?

FIRST EDITION
Copyright © 1991 by
Vernon Swenson

The text of this book may be copied up to and including five full pages without express written permission of the publisher provided the following acknowledgement
is given: "Quotation taken from WHAT CAN BE DONE? by Vernon Swenson. Used
by the permission of the author and Fairway Press." Permission requests to quote
more than five pages must be addressed to: Fairway Press, 628 South Main Street,
Lima, Ohio 45804.

7765 / ISBN 1-55673-363-1

PRINTED IN U.S.A.

Words of Appreciation

It is with gratitude that I present this book to the church. To the Lutheran churches of Tanzania and Liberia I say "Thank You" for the privilege of serving in their midst. It was in the Wembere Parish of Central Tanzania that I realized the need of an alternate model of ministry. One of my predecessors at Wembere, Pastor Douglas Lundell, introduced me to Roland Allen's book, *Missionary Methods: St. Paul's or Ours?* While teaching at the Mwika Bible School in Northern Tanzania the vision became clearer. At the Gbarnga School of Theology in Liberia I had the opportunity to briefly endeavor to establish a program of Theological Education by Extension. But the vision lives on, especially in my former student, Pastor Sumoward E. Harris.

While serving the parish of congregations in Wainwright, Czar and Hughenden in Alberta, Canada, the need in North America clarified and I wrote the first draft of this paper.

I also wish to thank my wife, Doris, who has given me so much assistance in editing and revisions. Her love and support have sustained me throughout my pastoral career.

Finally, thanks to the Lord of the Church for permitting me to be a servant of His church these 36 years.

Abstract

This book describes a model of pastoral ministry and education by extension which the author believes is practical, Biblical and necessary for the survival of many small Christian congregations in North America and elsewhere in the world. In other parts of the world the concept is usually known as Theological Education by Extension (TEE). The author has chosen to divide the concept into two parts — Indigenous, Bi-Vocational Ministry and Ministry Education by Extension (IBVM & MEE). Indigenous, Bi-Vocational Ministry (IBVM) deals with the call and ordination of laypersons for pastoral ministry and other forms of ministry in the church. Ministry Education by Extension (MEE) deals with the training of those persons called to pastoral and other forms of ministry. While the development of these two programs is most urgent for many small congregations, the application of the same principles to new mission work and large congregations can readily be grasped.

This paper does not purport to be an exhaustive discussion of the material available nor does it intend to suggest that it is definitive. Many of the proposals may need further study and revision. Some of the interpretations of the Bible and history might be challenged. The intent of the paper is to be provocative — to stimulate questions and debate, to challenge us to innovative thinking as far as pastoral ministry is concerned and to challenge us to daring ventures in ministry. If some of these things are accomplished the author will feel amply rewarded. Comments, suggestions, even criticisms, are welcomed and please address them to me at the address below.

Vernon Swenson
Box 483
Chapman, Kansas 67431
Telephones: (913) 922-6971
            (913) 922-6272

Table of Contents

A Story

"Bill, it's so late. It's 11:30 p.m. Did you have a long council* meeting? Did you have car trouble? I was getting worried. Lately the council meetings have been of a decent length; you have been getting home around 10 or 10:30 p.m."

"No, the council meeting was not too long; actually it was over about 9:30 p.m. Yes, I did have a little trouble. Joe noticed that I had a flat tire. He jumped right in and helped me change it. I wish we had a few more people like him around here and in this church. It sure was a good thing when they moved in on the Johnson place a couple of years ago. They are such a fine family."

"Well, then what made you so late? Anything special at council meeting?"

"Yes, Pastor John resigned."

"Resigned? They have been here only three years! I can't believe it. I thought they would stay with us a long time. Why?"

"The same old reason — money."

"Money? Is that the only reason?"

"Seems to be, but really not the only one. He also mentioned that they would like to be nearer their families and he would like to be closer to a college so that he could enroll in some night courses to get special courses in counseling. Eventually he hopes to become a chaplain. But right now, money seems to be the real problem. We talked it over some and, as usual, he was open and honest about the whole deal. He said

---

*The author of this paper comes from the Lutheran tradition. Therefore, the terminology found in this paper will be that which is most familiar to him. Council will mean the local governing body of a congregation. Bishop will be the term used for the leader of the synod or national church. Synod stands for the group of congregations in a geographical area, such as state or region. Cluster is a small group of congregations in a geographical area. Church means the national church or denomination.

that they liked it here, they liked the people, they thought it was a good place to serve, but since the birth of their last child they just have not been able to make a go of it. They have had to borrow some money from his parents. I wish they would have told us. Some of us maybe could have helped them out a little, but you know how they are. They wouldn't have wanted us to do that. He also said that they didn't feel like they wanted to apply for food stamps or something like that. Most likely they wouldn't be eligible anyway. So — they feel that it is best they make the move now.''

"Where are they going?"

"To a small town on the outskirts of Large City. Not a big church, but the community is growing. They will be only 25 miles from her folks. I guess the church is doing quite well. He will have a part-time secretary."

"Well, what are we going to do now? It seems that we can never get anyone who will stay here. The last one stayed only two and a half years. We didn't feel so badly to see them go since they never seemed happy here anyway. We weren't too happy with them either. His sermons were always about some social action business. Never a simple sermon just based on the Bible reading for the day. And she, well, it just seemed she did not care to mix much with us. I remember the old days when Pastor Johnson was here. He stayed 24 years. But that wasn't good either. The last years he just wasn't able to keep up with things, especially after we joined up with Zion. The two congregations were just too much. But now both of the congregations have gotten smaller and again it seems that we can't make it go any longer. I wonder how it is going for the Johnsons anyway. The last I heard she wasn't at all well. With the low salary they got for all of those years, inflation and everything, they must not have much. Social Security won't be much for them. Too bad we weren't able to pay the Social Security for them. At least we could have paid the four percent on the church pension fund, and then they maybe could have put that money aside for extra things. It's just too bad . . . Well, what did they say afterwards?''

"A lot of things. After Pastor John went home we stood out by the cars talking quite awhile. I suppose they wondered what we were talking about. They must have looked out and seen the cars still by the church. Well, Mary said that if we were all tithers perhaps we could get along for awhile. But you know how that is. If you start to push tithing that way — just to raise a preacher's salary, people won't like that and some of them will quit. Tithing is something that you want to do. We have always thought it was a good thing, but there aren't many who even try. This idea of proportionate giving and growth giving is better, but that takes time. Things have improved a little this past year. But not enough. We are some behind on our pledge to synod for general mission work of the church. Last week Lucy noticed a spot on the roof in the entryway. The steeple roof must be leaking again. I'll have to check that out soon."

"Was that all that was said?"

"No. Fred said that they had heard that the pastor down at Big Bend is going to retire and maybe we could join in with them. But I just don't see how that could hardly work. There are two congregations in that parish also. That would make a parish about 60 miles across! You just can't have four services in a Sunday morning. To get in three services it would mean that someone would have to have an 8 a.m. service and most likely the last one would be about 11:30 a.m. No one would like that. And on top of that someone would have to have an afternoon service or two congregations would have to go to every other Sunday. That is a sure way to kill a congregation."

"Well, is that all?"

"Someone suggested that we could maybe put the four congregations together and get a husband and wife team — for about one and a half salary. Sometimes I hear that they have a hard time finding places for the husband and wife teams. Usually big congregations do not have two vacancies, and if you get a husband and wife team, when they resign you all of a sudden have two holes to fill. And about the one and a

9

half salary business. I don't feel too good about that. If they are trained and ordained, they should both really be paid on salary scale. And where would they live? Most likely at Corner Junction. They have the best parsonage there. I sure would hate to see our old parsonage stand empty after all we did to fix it up. But it looks like that is what it will be. Corner Junction is 45 miles from here. Can you imagine having a pastor living 45 miles away? We wouldn't see them very often. Maybe just on Sundays, and we would still have to pay our full share of their salary."

"Did anyone mention getting a retired pastor? I understand that there are quite a few of them around."

"Yes, that was mentioned also and most likely will be talked over with the bishop. Susan is going to call the synod office tomorrow and talk with the bishop. Sure hope that synod can come up with something new and not just another recycling of the same thing. I just can't quite understand things. You know that big church in Megapolis? Well, that congregation used to be big. They closed down a couple of years ago and now another group has moved in there and has some kind of a church going in there. Can't see how they do it. And the Mormons, they moved into County City and built a big new church there. Don't think they have very many people there, but they sure have a nice building. Wonder where they get their pastors? You know, sometimes I think synod should go out to some of these places and ask them how they make it go. We maybe can't agree with all their teaching, but some of them do seem to have found ways to make things go. They must be doing something right or fooling a lot of people. I wonder what the Apostle Paul did. He sure seemed to start a lot of churches. I wonder where he got his preachers."

"Why don't you ask them? They ought to know."

"I might just ask the bishop when he comes down."

10

Introduction

The evangelical Christian church in America and its congregations face many challenges. The primary challenge that many small congregations face is maintaining ministry — just staying in business. During the past decades numerous Christian congregations have closed. This has left many communities without a Christian witness. The major reason has been economic, "We can not afford to pay the preacher." The closing of a congregation is a painful experience for everyone. It is extremely painful for devout members of the congregation. It is painful for the synod and the church. But it must be more painful for the Lord of the church who mandated that we are to go and make disciples. Disciples are made in congregations. Nearly without exception, it can be said that the closing of congregations is not the way to do mission. The problem is not unique to rural congregations. There are many urban congregations that had memberships in the hundreds a number of years ago and now are struggling to maintain ministry. There are also plenty that have closed down and their old buildings are now being used as karate houses or some such thing, or maybe just gradually crumbling, with broken windows and leaking roofs.

What can be done to maintain ministry in small congregations whether they be rural or urban? To pour more and more of less and less available resources into them most likely is not the answer. Something more innovative, creative and Biblical is needed. "Bi-Vocational Ministry and Ministry Education by Extension" is such a model.

The Christian church has a long established model of pastoral ministry. In most denominations it is college or university, seminary, a call to a parish and generally full-time employment by a parish. In many places this model has served the church well during the past decades. In many places it will continue to serve the church well. But it has not served the church well in other locations. Numerous defunct congregations are ample witness to that fact. To do a more aggressive ministry of mission we need more than one model of pastoral ministry. We need a model that will go hand in hand with the present model of pastoral ministry, augment it and enable small congregations to become truly self-governing, self-supporting and self-propagating. The author of this paper submits that "Bi-Vocational Ministry" and "Ministry Education by Extension" is such a model for pastoral ministry.

If Christian ministry, and specifically pastoral ministry, is going to be maintained in communities which currently have small congregations, the church has to face one difficult question, "How can it be done?" Can it be done with only our present model of pastoral ministry? Maybe even more germane is the question, "Should it be done using only our present model of pastoral ministry?" Assuming that the church has the resources of pastors and money to provide program support to hundreds of congregations that are now experiencing financial stress in maintaining their ministries, should the church make such program support generally available? Would program support that would have no visible end be the most healthy way to go? This author, from his experience, says "No."

To shore up ministry in congregations which have at one time been self-supporting with program support inherently has in it some detrimental factors. The first is that the congregations lose some of their feeling of identity, self-respect and self-worth, "At one time we were able to make a go of it, but we just can't seem to any more." Secondly, a certain amount of program control moves from the congregation to an office in a distant city. Any program changes that involve increased budgets must be approved by someone who is not next to the situation. Thirdly, recipient congregations are expected to complete seemingly endless forms that inquire into the "private" life of the congregation and submit those forms for somebody else's judgment. It is a great relief for a pastor to move from this kind of a situation to ministry in an autonomous congregation. Fourthly, the system is conducive to the exaggeration of reports so that they will look good and obtain favorable action by the department. Program support usually is not adequate to pay average, or above average, clergy salaries so it necessitates that the congregation be served by pastors who are on the low end of the salary scale. That might not necessarily be bad but it usually results in that congregations receiving program support have "revolving door" pastorates. Long term program support is not the best way to go.

Neither would denominationally equalized clergy salaries be the best solution for the situation in which small congregations find themselves. Equalized clergy salaries can be defended, but not for this reason. They can be defended on the grounds that they are a more Christian concept than our current system, and therefore more just. Equalized clergy salaries will not necessarily make ministry successful in small and declining congregations. One thing that equalized salaries will not do, at least not soon enough, is to increase the supply of pastors qualified to serve in many small congregations. To serve in small congregations can be a rather specialized form of ministry. All pastors are not gifted for small congregation ministry nor can they make the adjustment to it. A pastor who is very effective in a large congregation might be very frustrated in a small rural congregation.

What can be done? The first thing that needs to be done is for the church to recognize that as far as pastoral ministry is concerned it really has a problem. Secondly, it has to be willing to face the problem. The church's problem is basically with itself — "We have met the enemy and we have found him within." What can and must the church do?

The church will need to commit itself to change where change is necessary. The church will have to honestly say that our present one-track system of ministry is not adequate for the task of ministry that waits to be done. Therefore, we need an alternate model to go alongside the current model of pastoral ministry. If this is not recognized and done, the author of this paper is convinced that the church has only one other alternative: to continue to lose many small congregations and deprive many communities of a Christian witness.

Change is always threatening and sometimes frightening. It seems to be especially threatening to the church and specifically to the clergy. The writer first realized this clergy fear in Tanzania years ago. The church had few pastors and many evangelists. The pastors, African as well as missionary, usually served at the "station church" and the evangelists in the village churches. Many of these evangelists carried on very effective ministry with very, very low salaries, very little training and very little recognition. The church always wrestled with the questions, "What can we do to help them?" "How can we provide them with further training?" "How can we give them status?" "How can the church provide them with a more adequate standard of living?" Sometimes the evangelists themselves would raise the issues and request more training, more adequate compensation and a better defined status in the church. When this happened the response was exactly what it seems to be consistently throughout the world. Then the concern of the ordained clergy shifted. It shifted from how can we help evangelists to obtain that which we all recognize is necessary to a concern about protection of our own status. The worry became, "How far will this thing go? Will the time come when they will also want ordination?" And that is exactly the crux of the issue in the North American church and around the world. Are we as clergy willing to open the doors of "our club" so that others, with different backgrounds and training, may come in and the church be blessed?

It is indeed unfortunate, indeed lamentable, that we as missionary churches, sending missionaries to other lands, did not years ago turn back to the New Testament, turn back to Roland Allen, and realize that we need more than one model of pastoral training and ordination in the developing churches in other lands and also in our own churches at home. It is indeed unfortunate that we are so threatened by any suggestion of change and, therefore, very reluctant to change, even though the need

14

might be very evident. For its own welfare, does the evangelical church in America dare to advocate an alternative model of pastoral ministry? Can we take that risk? Can we do less?

Indigenous, Bi-Vocational Ministry and Ministry Education by Extension is a threatening concept. Will it cause a decline in the seminaries? Will congregations opt for bi-vocational ministers and leave current clergy unemployed? Will it give rise to all kinds of heresies? Will the sacraments be abused? None of these things need to happen, nor should they happen. These were the kinds of fears that plagued "third world" churches as they faced Theological Education by Extension. The results have been quite the opposite. Where TEE has been faithfully used, the church has grown, and because the church has grown, there has been an ever greater need for fully academically trained pastors, seminaries have flourished, the church has been faithfully instructed and the sacraments rightly administered.

By now, I believe, the case for the rightness and urgency of an alternate model of ministry has been adequately established. Let us move on.

Indigenous, Bi-Vocational Ministry

Joseph Sittler, in *Gravity and Grace*, maybe unintentionally and unknowingly, makes a powerful appeal for IBVM when he writes: "My questions led me further to ask what actually constitutes the church. It is constituted by two things that do not come out of history, society, human religion, philosophical reflection on ultimate issues or any human desire or intention. Those two things are Word and sacrament: the gospel as it is transmitted, and the gospel as it is celebrated in the dominical sacraments of the Lord's Supper and Baptism.

"The ordained ones — priests, pastors or ministers — also cannot be other than that which constitutes the church. Therefore I arrived at this conclusion: The ordained ones are the tellers of the story without which the church was not, is not, and cannot continue. They are those who tell the story of those events, promises, and mighty deeds of God that constitute the church.

"But cannot others tell the story? *The church must keep its story going and assure that there will never be a time or place where the sacraments commanded by Christ are not proferred.* (Italics mine.) Therefore the church insists on preparing a designated cadre to see to it that the constitutive story is told, and the nurturing sacraments are administered.

"This is a way of defining the ordained pastorate of the church that does not elevate it above the laity, but gives it a particular job among the people of God."[1]

In the above Joseph Sittler insists on two things. He insists that there must never be a time or place that the church does not preach the Word and administer the sacraments. Secondly, he insists that the church must prepare a designated cadre to see that the Word is preached and the sacraments are proffered. How is our performance measuring up to these two

17

absolutes? Are new congregations being established so that the gospel is responsibly being offered in all communities? Are all ethnic groups being reached with the result that self-governing, self-supporting and self-propagating congregations are being established amongst them? Are the residents of our changing inner cities being ministered to? The reality is that we are not doing these things as we ought to be doing them. Both our financial resources and our pastoral supply are too constrained to permit the maintaining of present ministries and aggressive evangelization. Our current model of pastoral ministry is not adequate for the task. However, Dr. Sittler's statement, "The church must keep its story going and assure that there will never be a time or place where the sacraments commanded by Christ are not proferred," is central. We wish that Dr. Sittler were still with us so we could ask him, "Just how do you think that can be done?"

But it can be done, and it must be done. From the time of Pentecost until Constantine the Christian church established and pastored congregations from England to India. In those congregations the story was told and the sacraments administered. How did that all come about? Was it by establishing new missions with great financial outlays? Was it not done largely through indigenous, bi-vocational ministry? Just what is IBVM and how can it work today?

I first became intrigued with the concept of indigenous, bi-vocational ministry in 1960-61 while serving as parish pastor at Wembere in Central Tanzania. I was pastor of a parish with several congregations. This was not an unusual situation. One pastor could have a parish of anything from one to 10 or more congregations. I soon came to realize that there were many times and places "where the sacraments commanded by Christ" were not being made available to the people except on very rare occasions. The evangelists serving in the "out-district" chapels led worship services and preached the Word as they understood it with their very meager training. However, they were not permitted to celebrate the Lord's Supper with their congregations, so those Christians were being denied the full benefits of the Gospel.

18

While serving under those conditions I was reading Roland Allen's classic, *Missionary Methods: St. Paul's or Ours?* and I came across the concept of indigenous, bi-vocational ministry. For me it was a life-changing experience. It revolutionized my thinking about Christian pastoral ministry. For years I had been admiring and defending "our method" of doing ministry and then I came to realize that in many ways our methods were not Biblical, not economically sound, not culturally adapted to the people and often not too successful. The Apostle Paul shows us another way. Please bear with me while I quote several paragraphs from Allen's book. We recognize that it was written with China, India or Africa in mind, but the church is pretty much the same around the world and its needs are the same — Word and Sacraments. All we need to do is transpose some images of time and place to our own church to find that it fits our situation nearly perfectly.

"Finally, St. Paul was not content with ordaining one elder for each church. In every place he ordained several. This ensured that all authority should not be concentrated in the hands of one man. It ensured the possibility of frequent administrations of the Sacraments. The infant church was not left to depend for its spiritual sustenance upon the weakness of a single individual. Responsibility was divided and many were enlisted in the service of the church. Thus the whole body grew together. As the general knowledge increased, the older men died, and the younger men, who had grown up in the new generation and shared their education and experience, gradually took their place and became the natural leaders and the ordained successors of their fathers, whilst young teachers who had a gift for preaching found their opportunities and their experience in the open services of the church.

"In our day, on the contrary, there has been a tendency to concentrate all function in the fewest possible hands. The same man is priest and teacher and administrator, sometimes architect and builder as well. We have set up a purely artificial standard of learning as necessary qualification for the ministry. We have required a long and expensive college

19

education as a preparation even for the office of deacon. We have taken the youngest men and trained them to occupy the position of authority, such very limited authority as a native may exercise under the supervision of a foreign priest-in-charge.

"The examination test is made the real test of fitness for the priesthood. Moral qualifications may suffice for the office of catechist, but if a man is to proceed further he must pass an examination of a very artificial character. In other words we select by examination. That system has long been tried, and is already being seriously questioned at home, and it does not seem to appeal to oriental minds as reasonable. In an address presented to the Lieutenant-Governor by the leaders of the Muslim community of the Punjab in 1904, they said:

> We presume that you English had your reasons for imposing such tests: we do not know and cannot guess them. The system is repugnant to old traditions, and we cannot consider the results of examinations as furnishing sufficient evidence of a man's aptitude to govern or to dispense justice. Our history has shown us that there are other criteria. To cursory examinations, in which memory plays a predominant part, we prefer the presumptions which arise on social position of the candidate, the services rendered to the State by his family, his own character and demeanour, and his aptitude to obey and command.

"Of course in our selection of candidates for Orders, we do not rely wholly on examinations. The candidate must bear a good moral character. But the fact remains that we have made too much of the intellectual test. That objection has been repeated by many missionaries — not only evangelistic, but educational. When we are constantly engaged in criticising the method of our Civil Governors in such a matter as this, it seems absurd that we should continue to imitate what we so often condemn.

"Four very serious consequences have followed upon our action:

"(1) The people have been deprived of the Sacraments. Our mission priests have often large numbers of communicants scattered over a very wide area, entirely dependent upon them for the administration of the Sacraments, with the result that the people have opportunity to receive the Sacraments only at rare intervals. These priests have often under them many excellent and devoted catechists who cannot be ordained, solely because they have not had a college education. Thus we deny the Bread of Life to people whom we teach to believe that partaking of the Bread of Life is the first duty of the Christian, and the first necessity for spiritual growth. It requires no great education to be able to celebrate the Holy Mysteries. We have put intellectual qualification in the first place, with the result that the congregations starve whilst we educate a few young men."

"(2) The young men so educated are sometimes, by that very education, out of touch with their congregations. They return to their people with strange ideas and strange habits. They are lonely, and they have to struggle against the perils of loneliness. They are not even the best teachers of people from whose intellectual and spiritual life they have so long been absent. They do not know how to answer their difficulties or to supply their necessities. They know so much Christian doctrine and philosophy that they have forgotten the religion of their country. The congregation has not grown with them, nor they with the congregation. They come, as it were, from, outside, and only a few exceptional men can learn to overcome that difficulty."

"(3) The grave men of the church, the natural leaders of the village life, and the natural leaders of the church are silenced. The church is not led and administered by the people to whom all would naturally turn, but either by a foreigner, or by a young man who has come with a foreign education. In this way a great source of strength is lost. The real elders of the community are not elders in the church, and the whole church suffers in consequence."

"(4) The natural teacher, the divinely gifted preacher, is silenced. The only teacher is the foreign-educated minister. There is no opportunity for the church to find its prophets,

21

nor for the prophets to find themselves. The prophet is in danger either of losing his gift or of leaving the church in order to find opportunity for its exercise."

"This is not to say that there is no place for the foreign-educated teacher. He may be said to resemble in some respects the young ministers whom Saint Paul educated in his own society by constant association with himself. Carefully selected and diligently trained, these men might go about as preachers and teachers of deeper truths and high knowledge, the messengers of, and fellow workers with, the white missionary, who, relieved of the overwhelming burden of personal ministration to numbers of small congregations over a vast area, could constantly be in touch with his churches, and yet have opportunity to open up new centers of work. It is absolutely essential that the founder of churches should keep in close touch with the communities which he has established, so that he may be able at any moment to intervene in any crisis or serious difficulty which may arise. Saint Paul needed Timothy and Titus, and we sorely need zealous and capable lieutenants whom we can despatch with haste to any point of our mission where the less educated and less trained leaders may be in danger of falling into error. We need such fellow workers not only to help us in directing the infant communities; we need them also to help us in breaking new ground. It is in working with them in evangelistic tours that we can best train them both before and after they leave college, and in evangelistic tours they may be of great service in instructing inquirers.

"Four things, then, we see Saint Paul deemed necessary for the establishment of his churches, and only four. A tradition or elementary Creed, the Sacraments of Baptism and the Holy Communion, Orders, and the Holy Scriptures. He trained his converts in the simplest and most practical form. He delivered these to them. He exercised them as a body in the understanding and practice of them, and he left them to work them out for themselves as a body whilst he himself went on with his own special work. He was ready at any moment to encourage or direct them by messenger, by letters, or by personal visits, as they needed direction or encouragement but he neither desired, nor attempted, to stay with them, or to establish his ministers amongst them to do for them what he was determined that they must learn to do for themselves. He knew the essential elements, and trained his converts in those and in those alone, and he trained them by teaching them to use what he gave them."[2]

This passage by Roland Allen is pregnant with many, many ideas and concepts that are valid and worthy of our noting and discussing. We will pick up some of them later in this paper, but now let us move on to a further discussion of "Bi-Vocational Ministry."

Indigenous, Bi-Vocational Ministry is not to be confused with what we commonly call "lay ministry" even though the ministers in IBVM may most often be lay persons. In the church the term, "tent making ministry," has often been used to describe bi-vocational ministry. Paul and his co-workers were bi-vocational in that they supported themselves by making tents while at the same time being engaged in evangelism and the establishment of congregations. In the context of this paper indigenous, bi-vocational ministers are lay persons who have been called, trained and certified for specific ministries in the church for a specified time and in a given location. The meaning of indigenous as used in this paper is, "produced, growing, or living naturally in a country or climate." (Webster's Collegiate Dictionary) Is not this exactly the model of ministry that we need in our congregations and communities — produced right there, growing right there, and living naturally right there? Indigenous, bi-vocational ministers — pastoral, educational, youth — are indigenous residents of the community and obtain their primary means of livelihood from the resources of the community while being members and ministers of a congregation. They most likely would be persons who have been born and reared right in the community within which they serve, but they also might be persons who have moved into the community and have identified themselves with the community. They would not be persons who have moved into the community for the express purpose of serving a congregation in some form of ministerial service. Normally they would be lay persons, but conceivably they could be persons with full seminary training and ordained in the customary manner.

Indigenous, bi-vocational ministry is a scriptural concept of ministry. It stems as least from the days of Moses. Moses was wearing himself out hearing all of the cases of the people. Jethro, his father-in-law, came to him and told him that what he was doing was not good. Jethro counseled him to choose and appoint capable men as leaders of thousands, hundreds, fifties and tens on a permanent basis. "Moses listened to his father-in-law and did everything he said. He chose capable men from all Israel and made them leaders of the people, officials over thousands, hundreds, fifties and tens. They served as judges for the people at all times. The difficult cases they brought to Moses, but the simple ones they decided themselves." Exodus 18:24-26 (New International Version) It just might be that Jethro offered a better solution to "clergy burn-out" than anything we have come up with today.

Most of the great spiritual leaders of Israel were persons within whom the Spirit of God moved and they were effectively used without long periods of formal, specialized training in an academic environment. Gideon, Barak, David and Amos are just a few examples from the Old Testament. From the New Testament we find such examples as Jesus, his disciples and the first elders of the church. Paul is the exceptional exception. But Paul, the exception, devoted his life to the training of indigenous lay leadership. You never read of Paul writing to his churches with words such as these, "I will correspond with the leaders in Jerusalem, and if we can get program support you will have a pastor."

No! Instead, Paul preached and taught until a group of believers were gathered together, chose, or had them choose local leadership, commended them to the leadership of the Holy Spirit, and finally he continued to instruct them by letter and occasional visits or by sending some other trained person to them.

This model of indigenous, bi-vocational ministry needs to be implemented in our congregations. It is not foreign to us. The founding congregation of the Augustana Synod of the Lutheran Church had its beginning with this model of ministry. The early Swedish settlers in Jefferson County, Iowa, found everything pleasing to them except that they did not have a spiritual leader. The settlers called forth Magnus Hakanson, a shoemaker, to become their spiritual leader and under his ministry the "children were baptized, their youth were confirmed, and the Lord's Supper regularly celebrated, and worship was conducted according to the Swedish rite."[3]

Joseph Sittler gives us a more recent example of this. "For reasons of good order, an ordained minister presides at the Eucharist. But we must not make a theological principle out of a provision for good order. My father, trained in the Joint (Lutheran) Synod of Ohio, began his ministry on the West Coast. He got to the lumber camps only once every three months. A couple of the congregations wanted the sacrament every Sunday, so old Mike Royce administered it. He was a lumberjack. On the frontier we were theologically very direct about some things; and then later we invented all kinds of ways to excuse what would actually be appropriate."[4] In the church it is indeed amazing what we sometimes do! Wouldn't it be far better if the church, beginning now, would endeavor to identify what is needful and appropriate, legitimize it and encourage its use rather than wait until extreme necessity compels it to do so?

The concept of indigenous ministry has largely disappeared from the mainline Christian denominations in North America, and this to our terrible loss. Instead of affirming and establishing the indigenous ministry that brought congregations into being in most difficult circumstances, it seems every effort was made to replace indigenous ministry with a non-indigenous ministry. Instead of training the lay persons locally, the men and women who sensed the call of God to ministry were sent off to school far away from their homes for extended periods of time, and later assigned in another location. Persons who could not meet this criteria have simply been denied the possibility of becoming ministers of Word and sacraments. In addition some congregations have been denied having the Word and the sacraments proffered to them on a regular basis and because of this some have disappeared off the landscape. However, in this day at least some aspects of indigenous, bi-vocational ministry seem to be once again gaining a foothold.

When the writer was a boy, it was practically unheard of that a Lutheran pastor could hold any form of employment other than his pastoral call. Today's economic factors have changed that and some ordained pastors do have employment other than just that of the call of the church. The discussion and response paper produced by the Division for Professional Leadership of the Lutheran Church in America (now merged into the Evangelical Lutheran Church in America) contains some very challenging insights concerning pastoral ministry, including this quotation, "The current practice of remunerating pastors completely from the congregational resources is valid and is expected to be the norm for the future. Yet there are parishes which have need for Word and sacrament ministry which evidence responsible stewardship, but which simply cannot afford the total costs of a pastor's salary and related benefits. Often factors beyond the congregation's control, such as size of membership, age of members, social changes and economic conditions account for the fiscal limitations. These circumstances are manifest across the church and affect parishes in rural and remote areas as much as those in suburban and urban contexts. In some instances churchwide agencies are able to supplement pastors' compensation needs.

"The Lutheran understanding of the church's ministry gives priority to people. A full ministry of Word and sacraments cannot be calculated in terms of hours spent by pastors doing church-related things. And a full ministry of Word and sacraments is not compromised in principle if the ordained minister engages in an occupation apart from his or her call to serve a congregation. In fact there is a strong tradition in North

26

American churches for clergy to minister to parishes while also having other employment. Although accurate statistics are not available, that practice does occur in some instances in the Lutheran Church in America.

"The object is to provide effective and accountable pastoral ministry and leadership to and through congregations. When full remuneration can not come from the parish, special arrangements need to be made to assure accountability and effectiveness. Clergy who enter such situations need to be clear about the goals of the ministry to be rendered, disciplined in the use of time and energy, capable of sharing appropriate responsibilities with lay persons, and willing to work with dedication and adaptability. Because the ministry of the church is at stake, synodical involvement is necesary."[5]

The camel has his nose inside the tent! From the days that it was anathema for an ordained pastor to even think of employment in addition to his call from the congregation we have come to the place where it is being practiced. Surely the economic factor has been the major contributing factor in the change, but just possibly the understanding that it is Scripturally sound has also had its influences. At least it has not been shown to be inconsistent with Christian doctrine and practice.

The next logical step is that, wherever economic pressures are having an unhealthy influence on either the congregation or the pastor (and that is most everywhere), consideration should be given to the calling and training of lay persons for ministry. This can be a viable alternative for some of the thousands of pastoral vacancies in congregations in North America and around the world. This alternative also needs to be examined by congregations that have been forced into multiple congregation parishes, new missions, congregations that are depending on some kind of program support and larger congregations sensing the need to expand or enhance their ministry. This alternative makes it possible for small congregations to be independent, self-supporting and self-propagating units, and larger congregations to expand their ministry.

In summary, indigenous, bi-vocational ministry happens when the congregation identifies persons they know as having the Christian commitment and leadership qualities that are necessary in the congregation and recommends them to the synodical candidacy committee. The candidacy committee guides them in a course of continuing education by extension following the guidelines of the church/denomination. They are approved for call, terms of service are carefully defined, and finally they are ordained for specific ministries for specified periods of time and in specific places. Since the needs of congregations and candidates vary widely this model of ministry will need to be very flexible to meet the needs of both.

One additional facet of indigenous, bi-vocational ministry needs to be pointed out before we move on to another topic. Roland Allen points out that "Saint Paul was not content with ordaining one elder for each church. In every place he ordained several. It ensured the possibility of frequent administrations of the sacraments. The infant church was not left to depend for its spiritual sustenance upon the weakness of a single individual. Responsibility was divided and many were enlisted in the service of the church. Thus the whole body grew together."[6] When our churches adopt and begin to implement indigenous ministry congregations that now do not have a called pastor, or are locked into a multiple congregation parish, will find that they will have several pastors — maybe two for worship leadership and two for the preaching ministry. Then, as their ministry grows they will call others for ministries such as education or music. Also, as the program moves along they will need to train others for the pastoral and worship ministries to replace those who are currently active when their terms expire. We should not think of any limits to the possibilities of growth.

Making IBVM Creditable

What happens when the pastor attends the annual church convention and you have a "Lay Sunday?" What happens when the pastor is on vacation or is ill and you have lay Sundays? Don't these two things usually happen? (1) The attendance drops by about 30 percent to 50 percent. (2) You hear the report, "Mr. or Ms. had the service and he/she did right well." What do the two above responses indicate?

Does the drop in attendance indicate that in the minds of some ministry by lay persons does not have much credibility when it comes to worship leadership? Does it mean that there is a notion floating around that says ordination infuses something into clergy that lay persons do not have? Does it indicate that college and seminary training and academic achievement make a worship service more credible and the lack of them makes the service less credible? Does it reveal some lack of respect for fellow members in the congregation and inadequate appreciation of their worth? Or does it reveal that some of these people wanted to do something else a Sunday or two and to them this was an opportune time? [Lest I be misunderstood I add this comment. Members of a congregation, for their own enrichment, should have the privilege of visiting other congregations from time to time. The question is, "Should it be the Sunday the pastor is gone?"] Maybe this drop in attendance indicates that some or all of these ideas are prevalent in our congregations. All of them need to be examined.

The second comment that he or she did well also indicates some things. Does it show that some recognize that fellow members in the congregation have God-given talents and abilities that could be called forth? Does it show that there is scholarship and learning already in the congregation? Does it show that some people do recognize and appreciate the

29

ministry of fellow Christians no matter what their official status might be? Does it reveal that many of the members of the congregation, by their presence, have a real appreciation of their congregation and its ministry? I think that all of these positive things are shown.

The above indicates that lay ministry does and does not have credibility. Is it good that in the minds of some, lay ministry does not have much validity? Should that attitude be changed? If so, how can we go about it? Several things can be done.

(1) We can clarify terminology. We talk about lay service and lay ministry or ministry of the laity. In my understanding of the common usage of these terms within the church lay service is when lay persons lead worship services and ministry of the laity is the Christian ministry every Christian does every day in his or her normal activities. If these understandings of the terms lay service and ministry are correct it is then inappropriate to use either of them for what is being proposed in this book. To use either of them will only lead to confusion.

To clarify terminology it is usually easier to find new terminology than to try to pour new meaning into old terminology. Let us limit the use of the term "lay service" to those rare occasions when lay persons are called upon to lead worship services with little or no advance notice or preparation. Ministry of the laity or lay ministry are becoming better understood in the church and let us continue that process of education. We need new terminology to identify those persons who would derive most of their livelihood from "secular" employment and also serve in the church in special ministries on a short or a long term basis. There are at least two possibilities. Up to this point in this book I have been using "Indigenous, Bi-Vocational Ministry." A shorter form, "Bi-Vocational Ministry" might be preferable for general usage. The word "indigenous" has been used deliberately to stress the point, that for this model of ministry, local people are used to perform the ministry, thereby eliminating the need to bring in strangers from a distance. This is an important concept that is consistently made by Roland Allen and also by the Apostle Paul. John D. Sutherland in his article, "Models for Pastoral Training" printed in "Lutheran Partners," used the name "Bi-Vocational Ministry."[7] Many people these days are bi-vocational; that is, they have two vocations. Therefore, this terminology can easily be assimilated by the church.

(2) The church needs to clarify what it means by ordination and who can be ordained. Currently we have a very restricted understanding of ordination. Generally speaking, only persons who have completed eight years of post high school academic training and have a call from a congregation to pastoral ministry or from the church to some special ministry, can be ordained. Is academic training one of the primary criteria for ordination? It would seem so. If that would have been the case in the times of Jesus where would the 12 apostles of Jesus have fit into the picture? If that would have been the case during the days of the Apostle Paul where would most of the bishops (pastors) of the first century church have fit into the picture?

Can there be ordination for ministries other than pastoral? How about ministry of music? How about ministry of learning? If a Christian is called by a congregation to give music and worship leadership on a part or full time basis can he/she be ordained? Just what is ordination? Is ordination the church calling and setting apart of a committed Christian for a specific function in the church? Is it as narrow as pastoral ministry? Can ordination be more inclusive than it currently is?

I believe that we have become rather paranoid when it comes to ordination. The author recalls an incident from his seminary days at Augustana Theological Seminary in Rock Island, Illinois. In a very small town a few miles south of Rock Island some Christians felt that they needed a church. They got together and formed an independent congregation and refurbished an old church building into a very attractive place of worship and called a local resident, who was employed in a factory in Moline, Illinois, and attending Augustana College, to be their pastor. This man had been ordained, in a public

31

service, by another independent congregation. At Thanksgiving time this friend of mine invited me to come to his congregation and preach. While conversing he told me his story in words something like these, "I feel that my ordination is as valid as anyone's." But the mere fact that he said this indicated to me that he must have been receiving some feedback suggesting that his ordination was somehow inadequate. Was my assumption right or was it wrong?

(3) The church needs to say that bi-vocational ministry is a valid model of ministry and in no way inferior to our present model of ordained ministry. In fact we might say that in some locations it is a more viable form of ministry. *An alternate form of ministry will never become accepted by the congregations until the church has clearly said that it is valid and has taken the pains to so instruct the entire church.* This will require some revision and clarifications in the constitutions of our churches. It will also require an enlarged understanding of the role of seminaries and other institutions of learning in the preparation of the servants of the church.

(4) The church will need to set up procedures to make bi-vocational ministry a viable possibility. This will be dealt with in other parts of this book.

Ministry Education By Extension

Ministry Education by Extension is the hand-in-hand companion of Indigenous, Bi-Vocational Ministry. We are becoming increasingly familiar with the concept of Theological Education by Extension (TEE) through articles in the church press and through reports of missionaries serving in global missions. Ministry Education by Extension (MEE) is the same concept, only with a broader perspective. TEE focuses strictly on theological education. MEE would have a wider focus — theological, liturgical, educational, administrative, evangelistic. In fact, it would provide nearly as broad a focus as a seminary.

MEE could accomplish for the church what is impossible to accomplish with our present pattern of four years of college followed by three years of seminary and most likely another year of internship. This pattern of training effectively eliminates many, if not most, potential lay leaders from further training before they have even had the opportunity to start. Many are simply not in a position to enroll at academic institutions for several years. Many persons who would like to serve the church as pastors, teachers or worship leaders have family commitments that simply make it most difficult, if not impossible, for them to be away from home for extended periods of time or to uproot their families two, three or more times to meet present qualifications for ordination. Many also do not have the financial resources to do it, and it appears that the church is not in a position to provide those resources. Therefore, because of our narrow, inflexible, one track pattern of training, the church has denied itself, and continues to deny itself, the abundant blessings that a broader concept could bring. Ministry Education by Extension could change all of this. Persons who feel the call of the ministry could be trained, pulpits could be filled, new missions started and devoted persons could even have supplemental income through their service to the church.

Ministry Education by Extension is a concept that is as old as the New Testament and maybe much older. An interesting prototype is found in 2 Chronicles 17:7-10, "In the third year of his (Jehoshaphat) reign he sent his official Ben-Hail, Obadiah, Zechariah, Nethanel and Micaiah to teach in the towns of Judah. With them were certain Levites . . . and the priests Elishama and Jehoram. They taught throughout Judah, taking with them the Book of the Law of the Lord; they went around to all the towns of Judah and taught the people." (NIV) Paul used the concept most effectively. Let us try to reconstruct the scene. Paul visited a community, preached, and taught for some weeks, maybe months, until a body of believers was gathered together. In most cases local leadership was appointed before he left, but not always. Sometimes they were chosen after he left (Acts 14:23; Titus 1:5). He commended the new congregations to the Lord in whom they had put their trust and went on his way to establish other congregations. What a daring thing to do — commend a group of new believers to local leadership, the Word of the Lord, and the guidance of the Holy Spirit! Problems did develop. Problems always develop where there is life. But Paul did not leave those congregations without help. He dealt with the problems. He wrote them letters which were read, reread, studied, discussed and passed around to other churches. On occasion he paid a personal visit to them, and at other times he sent trusted co-workers to them. That was effective MEE. By this method congregations had trained pastoral leadership. They became independent and self-supporting, and self-propagating. This, coupled with indigenous, bi-vocational ministry, was a most effective model of ministry. In the space of about 60 years the gospel was spread from India to England, and it began to have dramatic effect in bringing about vast social changes for the better throughout the whole social structure.

However, certain concepts of education by extension have persisted in the church. Martin Luther, in the writing of his catechisms, was in actuality using a form of Ministry Education by Extension. He perceived that parents and pastors were inadequately trained to transmit the Christian faith to those to whom they were responsible. In response to this need he wrote his catechism and other documents. John Wesley did essentially the same in the development of Annual Conferences and study courses for preachers, "for even if they were 'unlearned and ignorant men' who were being sent out with the Gospel, there was no reason why they should remain ignorant. Later he assembled them on different occasions so that they should be even better equipped for their task, and they would sometimes apply to him for help."[8] Even today our churches have extension courses and seminars here and there. But we do not have anything with a wide scope that is targeted so that congregations that cannot afford resident pastors can have pastoral leadership on an ongoing basis. How can this be done?

The Federated Parish: Let us visualize this situation. In an area, rural/urban or a combination of both, within a radius of about 50 miles there are congregations that do not have resident pastors, there are congregations that do have pastors but the congregations are struggling to maintain them, and there are large congregations with one or more pastors, but those pastors are overworked and frustrated. About 10 or 12 of such congregations could join together in a federated parish and call at least one, maybe on occasion more than one, fully trained pastor to be their teacher/trainer for MEE. Joining together these congregations could accomplish what it would be impossible for any one of them to do. Since the first step has to be made by someone, initially all congregations of one denomination in a chosen area would be invited to participate in this venture. But where a spirit of cooperation is evident, and the level of trust is adequate so that Christians can mingle together without being too threatened, this federated parish could embrace several denominations. Ecumenism would become a reality, starting at the grassroots and working its way up through the whole church.

The Students: The congregations also will carefully select candidates for the MEE program. Each congregation will need to select at least two persons — one for the preaching ministry and one for the worship leadership. Preferably they would select at least two for each of these responsibilities. The pastor/teacher would have at least two classes, a preaching class and a worship class, with about 20 students enrolled in each. These students would be beginning their ministry of preaching and worship leadership as they are learning. As the program develops the curriculum would be expanded. Their classes would not only be theoretical, but intensely practical.

The Pastor/Teacher: The pastor who would be called for this specialized ministry would of necessity need to be one who could effectively teach persons of all educational levels, relate well to persons without being overbearing, and above all committed to the concept of MEE. This pastor/teacher could currently be on the faculty of a seminary or be added to the roster of a seminary faculty as one engaged in Ministry Education by Extension. The pastor/teacher's responsibilities will be nearly exclusively to his/her students. Only on very rare occasions will he/she lead a worship service or preach. But it will be his/her concern to visit the congregations where the students are serving, observe their work there, meet with the special committee that will be overseeing the program locally, and give much encouragement. This will truly bring the seminaries in touch with the congregations.

Education by Extension: The task of the pastor/teacher will be to train leadership for all of the congregations in the federated parish. He will do this through a method of instruction that we will call "Ministry Education by Extension." In many third world countries it is called "Theological Education by Extension," but I have preferred to use the term, "Ministry Education by Extension" because of its wider scope. In this method of education he/she will use especially prepared programmed textbooks which the student will study in his/her home. Then every two to four weeks the entire group will meet together, discuss the work they have done, share experiences they have had in their parish ministries, leave their work with their teacher for correction, and receive new assignments. This is not the same as a correspondence course in which the student receives a course of study from the college or university, completes the lessons at home, returns them to the school for correction, does another and keeps on doing that until the course is finished without ever seeing the instructor once. Ministry Education by Extension will keep the student in touch both with the teacher and the parish he/she serves. Also MEE will keep the instructor in touch with the student, the parishes and the seminary where he/she is a member of the faculty. I suggest a radius of 50 miles around the extension center so that students can make a round trip in an evening without too much time being spent on the road.

Just think of the impact in our evangelical churches when we have many MEE centers staffed by teachers who are a part of the faculties of our seminaries!

Resources: This pastor/teacher would not do all of this work alone. On occasion he/she would plan seminars, maybe involving several MEE centers, and bring in persons gifted in particular areas of ministry. An example could be counseling. Also in this day and age we have a wealth of materials in addition to textbooks. We have VCRs and video, telenet, satellite television, telephones, cassettes, duplicating machines, etc. All of these instructional aids could broaden the experience of the students.

We are not without models to look to for guidance in the implementation of such a program. Numerous churches in the "Third World" have used the program effectively. We have missionaries who have worked in TEE. We have seminaries that have been leaders in the development of TEE. Books, many of them, have been published. The time has come for us to gather together all of our available resources, share them and out of them develop new and better teaching materials. Narrow provincialism which says, "This is ours and we will not share," should not be found in the church. We exist to assist and enrich each other. The time has truly come for us to learn from our overseas partner churches, and each other, not just talk about it.

Implementation of the concept of IBVM and MEE need not be unduly taxing on the resources of the church or life-threatening to the church. The program will need to be carefully developed and goals clearly defined. Implementation will have to be gradual with full cooperation of the church, bishops and congregations involved. You may not at any one time find eight or 10 pastoral vacancies in the radius of 50 miles from a projected extension center. However, the program can start with a smaller group of congregations. Then, as more congregations become interested and pastoral vacancies occur, the number of congregations enrolled would be increased. To facilitate the implementation of Ministry Education by Extension there may need to be some relocation of pastors. However, this should not be insurmountable. Usually there are pastors, especially in small congregations, who desire a move and could be encouraged to make such a move without too much dislocation of their lives. The move might even result in the betterment of their lives and ministries.

The Congregations: At the congregational level something like the following would have to happen. Let us consider a parish that now has two congregations yoked together and served by one pastor. These are small congregations having a tough time making a go of it and the pastor is underpaid. The congregations are gradually declining in membership so the writing is "on the wall." Either they will have to bring a third congregation into the parish to make it go for a little longer, go to something like a supply pastor ministry, or go out of business. Their pastor is recently out of seminary, or he might have a number of years of experience but has never received adequate salary increases, so the salary packet is honestly inadequate.

Assuming the entire salary packet, which includes medical, auto allowance and all other allowances, currently is $26,000. From this we can project a budget something like this. The annual budget of $26,000 divided by 52 makes a weekly cost of $500 for the two congregations or $250 for each congregation for pastoral care. Out of that $250 you would first take $80 for worship leadership — $50 for the preacher and $30 for the worship leader. That would leave a balance of $170. From that you would take $75 for the extension center pastor/teacher, leaving $95. The $75 multiplied by 52 weeks and by 10 congregations would give the pastor/teacher an annual salary packet of $39,000. This would mean that each congregation could use the $95 weekly or $4,940 annually to cover such items as occasional pulpit supply, textbooks, travel to the extension center, and so on. Such items as rent for the extension centers would be very minimal since it would be anticipated that church facilities already available would be used. In addition, we would anticipate that the national church would invest something in the ministry just as we currently invest in program support of our congregations and new missions. The following is how a budget comparison of budgets for the two models of ministry might look.

Budget Line:	Present Budget for 2 Cong.	Present Budget for 1 Cong.	IBVM & MEE for 1 Cong.	IBVM and MEE for 10 Cong. Fed. Parish
Pastor's Salary	$14,000	$7,000	$4,160	$41,600
Worship Leader/ Liturgist			1,560	15,600
Housing	3,000	1,500	480	4,800
Pension Fund	2,700	1,350	800	8,000
Medical Insurance	3,000	1,500		
Continuing Education	300	150		
Auto/Travel in parish	3,000	1,500	1,000	10,000
Extension Center				
Pastor/Teacher			3,900	39,000
Pulpit Supply			200	2,000
Books/Supplies			400	4,000
Travel to Extension Center			500	5,000
TOTALS:	$26,000	$13,000	$13,000	$130,000

It will take commitment to get a visionary project such as this off the ground. But maybe we have only one of two choices — either to make the commitment or continue to see the decline in our congregations. The following is a diagram illustrating the flow of MEE supervision and instruction.

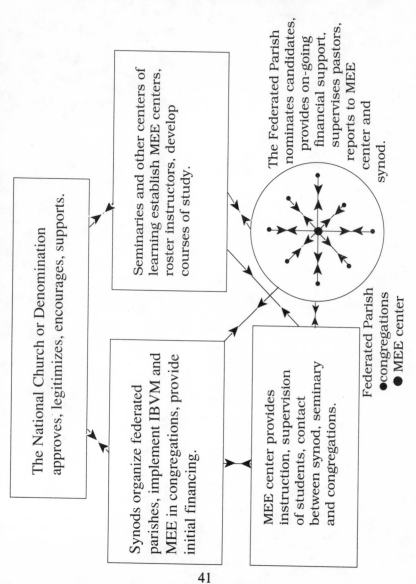

The National Church or Denomination approves, legitimizes, encourages, supports.

Seminaries and other centers of learning establish MEE centers, roster instructors, develop courses of study.

The Federated Parish nominates candidates, provides on-going financial support, supervises pastors, reports to MEE center and synod.

Synods organize federated parishes, implement IBVM and MEE in congregations, provide initial financing.

MEE center provides instruction, supervision of students, contact between synod, seminary and congregations.

Federated Parish
● congregations
● MEE center

IBVM
and
Practical Ramifications

There are some very practical concerns with which the church needs to deal as it approves and develops a concept of indigenous, bi-vocational ministry. I shall endeavor to identify some of them.

Selection of Candidates: How do we currently go about the selection of our candidates for pastoral ministry? Isn't the initiation of the selection primarily a decision on the part of the individual who will ultimately be ordained? Indeed, pastors and others in the congregation may encourage individuals, especially young people, to consider the Christian pastoral ministry, but usually no action is taken until the individual himself/herself comes forward and makes his or her intention known. At the initial stages there is little or no involvement of the congregation of which the individual is a member. In fact, is there ever much significant involvement by the congregation in the whole process of selection and training of candidates for pastoral or other ministry? A few years ago a seminary wrote to me requesting a letter of recommendation concerning a young individual who was enrolled in the seminary and supposedly a member of the congregation I was serving. I had to reply to the seminary that I was really not able to give a letter of recommendation since I had never met the individual even though the individual's name was in our church records. We hope that such extreme cases are very, very rare. In my own case I am not aware that my home congregation was ever contacted about my qualifications about becoming a pastor. Of course, that was 40 years ago, and I trust that procedures have improved a good deal since then.

From the Scriptures it would appear that the Apostle Paul would never have left the selection of pastoral leadership of the churches up to volunteerism. The early church indeed did have a good number of volunteers who went about from church to church. They called themselves "prophets." Without a doubt some of them were faithful ministers of the church (Acts 13:1-2, 1 Timothy 1:18). But others were not so commendable. Some came teaching false doctrines (Galatians 1:6-9, Acts 15:1); others were greedy for gain (1 Timothy 6:5). This raises the question of accountability. Both the faithful and the unfaithful servants of the church need someone to be accountable to. We all need this. This is exactly what Paul provided in his method of selection of candidates for pastoral ministry.

In bi-vocational ministry the local congregation in need of pastoral or other leadership would from its own midst call forth individuals for service. This would not be done lightly. A good deal of thought, time and prayer would be put into the process. The procedure could go something like this. A representative from the bishop's/president's office would visit the congregation and carefully instruct the council as to the qualifications and expectations of pastors. A small call committee could be formed and they would carefully consider every possible candidate in the congregation. The call committee would draw up a list of names and present the same to the council. The council would review the list and set up an interview process with prospective candidates. Those candidates who would respond favorably to the proposal of service would be interviewed by a representative of the synod/district's office and then their names would be forwarded to the congregation for the issuing of calls. Upon the acceptance of a call the candidate would begin a course of study by extension. The ideal would be that in each congregation at least two persons would be called for the preaching ministry and two called for worship leadership. The advantages of having several involved would be that the workload and responsibility would not fall so heavily on any one person's shoulders. They would have flexibility to schedule their pastoral responsibilities in and around other employment and other responsibilities. It is not uncommon for individuals to have a full-time job plus a part-time job. Bi-Vocational ministry could be a part-time job that would be a benefit to both the individual and the congregation because terms of service can be carefully drawn up. Is this to say that someone cannot "feel the call to the ministry" and respond by making that sense of call known? Of course not! Anyone sensing that God is calling him or her into the ministry should listen very carefully to the leading of the Holy Spirit and then let that sense of call be known to appropriate persons. The initial call can come either to the individual or through the committee, but either way the individual should go through the entire call process. We must be very careful not to set boundaries as to how God can call us.

Tenure: In our present system when a congregation extends a call to a pastor it is usually open-ended. It can be for life. It can go on and on without ever a pre-planned review or evaluation. The pastor can stagnate in his ministry and as long as nothing drastic happens most likely no one will venture to raise the question that his or her call and ministry needs to be reviewed. Most of us are aware of situations where pastors, at least according to conventional wisdom, have stayed too long. Most of us are also aware of situations where there has been questionable ethical conduct and no action has been taken or it has been taken only after serious damage has been inflicted on the congregation and on others. Most of us also know of pastors who "just were not cut out for the job" but who stayed on in the pastoral ministry just because they felt trapped and had no place to go. These situations are tragic and shouldn't happen often. However, it is very difficult to do otherwise with our current method of call and placement. Term calls might be a partial solution, but even then who wants to fire a pastor? Where will the pastor go? What will the pastor do? And in some cases, where will the congregation find another pastor?

IBVM could be at least a partial solution to some of these problems. In the first place the congregations would be calling persons they already know. The call committee would simply pass over incompetent persons as they review the

45

membership list. Not so in our present system. When a congregation comes to the calling of a pastor what do they really know about the candidate? Yes, they have a dossier but what does that really reveal? What applicant elaborates on his or her weaknesses in the résumé? How much does the bishop or his assistant really know? Is a bishop or assistant who is under pressure to get someone placed going to elaborate on the weaknesses of the candidate? Hardly. No need, the congregation will find them out in a few months.

Tenure is hard to build into the ordinary call. But, it could be a natural part of a call for bi-vocational ministry. Tenure would be stipulated in the terms of service — one year, two years, three years. Maybe a two-year term that could be renewable for a second term would be a good way to start. After the second term there would be a required rest of at least one year before a call could be extended again. This could be done without undue hardship since the pastor would already be employed elsewhere and he or she would have anticipated the review at the end of the first term, knowing that the call could not be renewed at the end of the second. This gives both the congregation and the employee a more graceful way of terminating service. If the pastor does not function too well the congregation could tolerate that for a period of time and at the end of the contract not renew the call. With experience, training and some encouragement the pastor might even improve.

This kind of a system of tenure would tend to insure that the congregation would continually be developing a qualified cadre of persons capable of leadership. Someone would have to be found to replace those whose terms expire. Some may say, "Some congregations just do not have qualified persons in their membership." That is simply not the case. In any group of 30 people we will find at least two persons who can function as song leaders, two persons who can teach, two persons who can speak in public, two persons who can lead a liturgy and so on. They are there. All that is necessary is that they be identified, trained and put to use. In the author's former congregation of 104 confirmed, communing, contributing members we had 44 persons who served as lectors (readers of the Scripture lessons). Granted, all of them were not accomplished readers, but all of them read so that others could understand and be blessed. Also, they were developing their skills by use. We also had several lay persons who had experience of worship leadership, sermon preparation and delivery. Only on very rare occasions was a sermon read in that congregation. God is generous in his distribution of talents and gifts to his church.

Discipline: Discipline of the clergy must be one of the most difficult things that a bishop of the church faces. In a congregation the pastor is often the last person to hear of misconduct of a parishioner. Most likely the pastor is a "newcomer" to the community and not really in on the "goings on" in the community. By virtue of office the pastor is somewhat isolated from the community. If this is true of the pastor, it also must be true of the bishop. Who in a congregation is going to report to the bishop? Most likely no one — until the problem blows up to such proportions that it can no longer be contained. This would not be very apt to happen with indigenous ministry. In the first place, it most likely would not happen because the congregation would intimately know the life and character of candidates before they are called. Secondly, responsibility for pastoral leadership would be shifted closer to the congregation than it now is. A congregation most likely would not tolerate misconduct very long. The reputation of the congregation is at stake. They would all know about the misconduct and most likely would take action on it; if not earlier, certainly when it comes time to renew the call. An offender simply would not be given a second time around.

In matters of exercising discipline we need once again to go back and see what Paul did with the first churches. Discipline problems the churches did indeed have. Plenty of them! But, contrary to what we do today, the responsibility of disciplinary action rested with the local congregation. Roland Allen writes, "In the case at Corinth we see Saint Paul's principle

47

of mutual responsibility again enforced, and he enforced it by staying away from Corinth until the church had realized and executed its duty, and had cleared itself of complicity in the crime of this offender.''[9] Can we imagine our bishops today taking that kind of an approach to disciplinary problems? We expect bishops to come and straighten things out for us. Following Pauline practice the bishop would reply, "You take care of the matter first and then I will come and visit you; and I won't come until you have made every effort. However, if you simply can not handle the matter I will do what I can to assist you."

Terms of Service: For Indigenous Ministry and Ministry Education by Extension to be successful detailed, explicit terms of service will need to be drawn up and reviewed periodically. The candidates will need to know as precisely as possible just what is expected of them and what is not expected of them. They will need to know what pay they will get and what assistance they will receive for their continuing education. The synod will need to give guidance in the drawing up of terms of service. In the terms of service there will be things that will be common to all situations and some that will be unique with each congregation.

Rotation of Responsibility: It would be very advantageous for the congregations to call at least two worship leaders and two preachers. It would be doubly advantageous if the two could have different types of secular employment. For instance, if one of the preachers could be a farmer and one could be a public schoolteacher that would be ideal. A farmer would find it difficult to find time for preparation during busy seasons on the farm, such as planting and harvesting times. A school teacher would find it difficult to find time for preparations during the first days of school, test weeks and the closing days of school. But between the two they could work out their own schedules to their best advantage. Since they would be paid by the week the schedule of remuneration would be no problem.

Other Pastoral Duties: What about such things as visitation of the sick and shut-ins, calling on prospective members, etc.? Most of these things could be picked up by volunteers. Provision will need to be made in the terms of service for such things as Holy Communion for those who can not get out for regular services. In some cases it might be advantageous to call and train a third person for these responsibilities.

Larger Congregations: Can Indigenous, Bi-Vocational Ministry and Ministry Education by Extension also work in larger congregations where there are one or more resident pastors? Certainly! Pastors of large congregations often complain of their overloads. What better way could there be than by calling and training lay persons to relieve some of the pressure? They might have to share a portion of their salaries but that should be a reasonable sacrifice for the reduced workload. Indigenous Ministry and MEE might really make small group ministries a viable possibility in many large congregations.

Ministry Education By Extension
and
Practical Ramifications

Even as the implementation of IBVM will have practical ramifications that the church will need to deal with, even so the implementation of Ministry Education by Extension will have ramifications which the church will need to resolve. At this point let us endeavor to anticipate a few of those.

Seminaries: As mentioned earlier in this book one of the first questions which will be raised will be, "What will happen to our seminaries? Won't enrollment drop and eventually won't some of them be compelled to close because the church can no longer afford to support them? Won't the quality of education go down as MEE centers are opened and students enroll in them for pastoral training rather than enroll in a regular seminary?" These are legitimate questions and only experience will afford us the certain answers.

As far as the fear of resident enrollment dropping the only guideline we have is what has been experienced in other seminaries where Theological Education by Extension has been practiced. It seems that in most cases resident enrollment has increased. The churches have grown with a consequent need for more full-time theological education. However, in this regard we must remember that our seminaries are already threatened. Some are having difficulty maintaining enrollment and most are having financial problems. So, if those probems should become more intense after the initiation of Ministry Education by Extension the blame should not necessarily be laid at the feet of the MEE program. It might be that some seminaries have completed their tasks and it is time to write over them "Ministry Completed." If that should happen that will indeed be a painful process, but from what I read in the church press it does seem to be a distinct possibility.

51

But let us think more positively. Instead of thinking of closing why not think in the terms of growth? For example, if we now have a seminary with a resident student enrollment of 350 students is there any good reason why the enrollment should not be 2,400 students? In the residential program there would be 400 and 2,000 in the extension ministries. Just think what such a development would mean to the life of the church! Think possibilities, not just maintenance.

As far as maintaining the quality of education is concerned I have no hard facts to support my assumption that it will not decline. All I do know is this. When the province of Alberta began its program of education by extension their experience was that the students who studied in the extension centers were not behind those who studied in the residential facility. In fact, the extension students consistently did better on identical tests than those in the residential education program. The reason that was given for this discrepancy was that those in extension centers were immediately putting to use what they had learned, while for those in the residential centers it was largely a theoretical education. Once again we will have to see what will happen, but I can envision how much more effective it would be to study sermon preparation knowing that you have to preach a sermon the coming Sunday instead of dreaming about the day you will be preaching after graduation.

Establishing New Congregations: Every denomination of the evangelical Christian church desires to experience growth through the development of new congregations. Populations are always shifting, new housing developments are built and new suburbs are developed. The gospel needs to be brought to these places through the development of new congregations. However, this sometimes does not happen. Why? We just do not have enough money. With our present single model of pastoral ministry it is very expensive to develop new congregations and we simply do not have enough money to maintain our current ministries and be aggressive in the opening of new ones. But, should our vision for new ministries be so constrained by the lack of money?

Can we imagine the Apostle Paul saying, "We should establish congregations in Corinth, Beroea and Rome but we just do not have the money?" Or can we imagine him further saying, "Even if we could establish these congregations how could we pastor them and get buildings for them?" It appears that such questions did not bother Paul. After gathering a group of believers together they had to fend for themselves under the guidance of the Holy Spirit, the Word, letters and an occasional visit. Incredible, but it worked!

Some few congregations are being developed today following methods similar to Paul's. We should do some aggressive research to find out just what is happening in those places and open ourselves up to learn from them. But what do we usually do? We send a mission developer into an area and hopefully, after the expenditure of a large amount of money for program support, a congregation is established and a building erected, with the result the new congregation is saddled with a large debt to pay off. Just the thought of being a part of paying off a large debt must be a deterrent to many prospective new members. As an example, let us say that by the time the congregation gets off of program support it has a membership of 150 members, an average of 100 at worship services, one pastor, and an annual budget of $60,000 and a debt of $250,000. Instead of that why not have four congregations, eight pastors, no buildings, no debt, modest budgets for home ministry and generous budgets for outreach ministries of all kinds? Which of the above two models would come closest to the model that Jesus must have envisioned?

Finances: If our churches would approve such an innovative concept of ministry as Indigenous, Bi-Vocational Ministry and Ministry Education by Extension how could we ever finance it to get it off the ground? Indeed it will cost some money, but it will cost more in dedication, commitment and vision than money. Part of the financing could come from a shift in the allocation of money from program support to MEE. We will need to develop courses of study and train pastors/teachers for the MEE centers. However, that should not

53

be such a major item in order to get a few pilot projects going. The MEE centers would be partially self-supporting from the beginning and later fully self-supporting. Also, it would be logical to expect that out of the centers we would see courses of study developed and experimented with. We are going to have to move away from our isolationism and begin working together as brothers and sisters in Christ. Things can be done modestly and with a limited budget. And lastly, the church is just going to have to come to grips with the need and find ways to underwrite it; maybe through designated gifts.

These are just a few of the practical concerns with which we will have to wrestle as we move into an innovative model of ministry. We will just have to do like Paul did — deal with the problems as they arise. And that is challenging!

Dealing With Our Fears

Change is always filled with fear. It seems that changes conjure up more fears in the church than any place else. This must be because the church is such a vulnerable organism. While "the gates of hell can not prevail against it," it is still so fragile. It must depend on the loyal support of its members for its life. If the members are offended they may fall away. If they are not nourished faithfully by Word and Sacrament, they will surely wither away. If they are not listened to they will withhold their support. If they feel that they are listened to, nourished and respected they will show an intense loyalty. So, when we suggest change we are gripped with fears. Some may be legitimate. Some may be unfounded. All need a sympathetic hearing and all need to be dealt with.

When such a radical change as proposing IBVM and MEE is suggested fears are bound to surface. The fears may be so strong that we are even unwilling to discuss the proposal. Another reaction might be to discount the whole idea and pass it off with "It will never work" or, "It might work some place else, but not here." Whatever the cause the fears need to be dealt with. The alternative of not dealing with them might ultimately be so tragic that we do not even want to speculate about the possibilities. If the evangelical church does not seriously consider indigenous, bi-vocational ministry and ministry education by extension now, most likely a golden opportunity will pass us by. At this point it is difficult to even imagine what fears might arise if this proposal is taken seriously, but let us try.

Clergy Fears: Those who will be most threatened and most likely most fearful of the indigenous, bi-vocational ministry concept of ministry and the ministry education by extension concept of training most likely will be the ordained clergy. The clergy might feel that they have the most to lose. Just what if, down the road 100 miles, several congregations band together, establish a federated parish and a MEE training center, call their own people to serve them, and it turns out that those congregations not only hold their own but make modest growth? What if the word gets around that some of those trained in the MEE centers are actually turning out to be very capable worship leaders and preachers? Will the result be that it will be hard for some pastors to get calls? Another result could be that it will be more difficult to move around in the church because there will be fewer vacant parishes. Will the result be that the bishop will suggest to me that I relocate because a federated parish is being formed and lay persons will be doing the ministry? These might be some very realistic fears.

If some of the above fears actually do become reality does that mean that we should hang on to our current one track model of ministry and not try indigenous, bi-vocational ministry? I hope not! I trust that we are better churchmen and churchwomen than that. We can not permit personal fears to stand in the way of the advancement of Christ's kingdom. We will need to deal with our fears. The church will need to deal with its fears. But how?

First, we will have to face the possibility that growth is possible and that there will be ample opportunity for relocation for all who desire new opportunities and who possess the pastoral qualities needed in the new opportunities. Secondly, maybe some of us clergy should consider a career change. Increasingly, persons who are entering our seminaries are second career people. That is good. On the other side of the coin it might well be that there should be an increasing flow in the other direction; maybe some clergy persons should be becoming second career persons in the secular world. They just might be very good leaven in the secular work place. Some might feel very relieved by their change in status. Maybe that burned out or stressed out feeling will be alleviated.

The church will need to take an active roll in the process of career changes. The only Christian thing to do now, and in the future, is to assist those who need to make a career change. Some of them have given many faithful years of service to the church; now the church in integrity can assist them in a career change.

Without a doubt some of our existing clergy will be apprehensive about the IBVM proposal. That will only be natural. We need to rise above that and see the possibilities.

Parish Fears: Some parishes will have fears even as the clergy will have fears. Some congregations are already threatened. They might feel that the proposal of indigenous, bi-vocational ministry and ministry education by extension will only hasten the process to their demise. Christians love their churches and one thing they certainly do not want to do is something that will hasten the day their congregation may no longer exist. Under our present system they maybe can survive a few more years with supply pastors or some such arrangement. If IBVM and MEE is suggested to them they may find themselves just unable to cope with the idea that one of their own could lead them in worship. In such a negative situation the recommendation of change might speed up the process of the death of the congregation. However, the illness was terminal anyway and this would sort of be like "pulling the plug" of the lifeline of support.

But congregations should not have undue fears. No congregation should be pressured into this model of ministry. If they are going to come in they will need to come in willingly and whole-heartedly. They will have to look on it as a new lease on life, a new opportunity to serve in the Kingdom. If congregations that are in the area where a MEE center is being formed do not wish to enter the federated parish they should have the opportunity to carry on their ministry as they have done in the past, but the door must always be left open, with a big welcome sign over it, for them to join. Indeed there are some congregations that will eventually pass off the scene, with or without indigenous, bi-vocational ministry. We should help them to gracefully write "Ministry Completed" over their closed doors.

Synodical Fears: Most likely the synods with their bishops and administrative officers will also have some fears. They will certainly need to be involved in the call process of indigenous, bi-vocational ministers and the establishment of MEE centers. That will mean extra work. But it may not be as much extra work as a change in work. Instead of a work of "patching fences" it will be a work of restoring ministries and establishing new ones. It will be a work to be excited about. The congregations will become increasingly self-supporting, self-governing and self-propagating. That will be a good day in the church!

Church Fears: Yes, there might even be some fears on the level of the national church bodies, but I really don't see why. Hopefully we are a resilient, progressive church that can be innovative and non-threatened by a few changes. With indigenous, bi-vocational ministry and ministry education by extension I can see how we can reach our goals of mission in North America and in the process also become a light and inspiration to the churches the Holy Spirit has led us to establish in other countries. Just think, when our sister churches in other countries see us using Indigenous, Bi-Vocational Ministry and Ministry Education by Extension they might well say, "The Mother Church is doing it and it is working there. Surely it will also work for us."

Property Fears: "If we cannot afford to pay the preacher can we afford to maintain the building?" Maybe "Yes." Maybe "No." To change our model of ministry will certainly raise questions about our buildings. "Will IBVM be appropriate in our building?" In many places it will be. In other places it may not be. But, we can ask the same question about current ministry in some of our buildings today. Questions about our buildings need to be raised no matter what model of ministry we have. The author of this book sees no reason why a building that is functional now should not be with IBVM. More will be said about this subject in "Reflections."

Fears. Yes, we all experience them from time to time, but we begin to live victoriously and joyfully when we overcome them and reach out to new visions and opportunities. May God, in his love, grant that to us.

Steps Toward Implementation

Providing this presentation of IBVM and MEE has been lucid enough and detailed enough so that we have some grasp of the idea, *what should we do next?* At this particular juncture in our life in the evangelical churches in America we do well not to bypass any idea about ministry without giving it at least a hearing. We have thousands of congregations in North America that do not have a resident pastor. The Evangelical Lutheran Church in America alone has over 900 pastoral vacancies and the projection is that the number is going to increase. We have overworked pastors. We have undercompensated pastors. We have struggling congregations. We have dying congregations. We will do well to seriously look at every option. With that in view I suggest the following steps.

Study: Several denominations in North America are currently engaged in some kind of study of ministry. We need to thank the leaders of the churches who have had the wisdom and insight to propose these studies. They really could not have done better. In our studies of ministry let us not look back too much upon the past. Indeed, we need the study of the past to gain perspective, but also we need to be looking to the future and asking hard questions about the needs of the church as far as ministry is concerned. Therefore, let us place this concept of ministry and training on the table with all of the other ideas and give it a fair hearing. Let it be discussed, challenged, revised and improved. In the future let there be reports that this concept of ministry has also been reviewed. At this point one needs to point out again that IBVM and MEE is not intended to be a substitute for our present model of ministry, but rather, it is intended to be a viable second alternative.

Discussion: Let us put Indigenous, Bi-Vocational Ministry and Ministry Education by Extension on the agenda for

59

discussion in all kinds of settings. Let it be discussed in our church press, at pastors' convocations, workshops, cluster meetings and synod assemblies. Let it be included in material for congregational study and reflection. Possibly our divisions or boards of education should prepare brief courses on ministry and elicit response from our congregations. Ultimately it is the congregations that have the most to gain or lose.

Pilot Projects: Let us establish some pilot projects in various parts of the country. If, after preliminary hearing it is found that there is nothing contrary to the Christian faith and nothing contrary to a good churchly understanding of ministry in the proposal, then let us move forward with some pilot projects. We might learn more from them than from reams of study papers. Funding for such pilot projects should not be too major a problem since the amount required would not be great. For guidance in the establishment of pilot projects we can turn to churches already engaged in such ministries.

Action by the Church: For IBVM and MEE to become an effective reality will require enthusiastic reception and action by the evangelical churches in their regular assemblies. This will take time to achieve, but the time spent in preparation will be well spent.

Cooperation: For the adoption of a second model of ministry in our churches there will need to be cooperation at all levels in the church. The cooperation of the bishops/presidents of our churches, our seminaries and other institutions of learning, our synods or districts and their leaders, the divisions for ministry, global mission, outreach and other divisions will be needed. The denominational magazines and other publications of the church will need to use their facilities for dissemination of information and encouragement of change. We must endeavor to seize every opportunity for the welfare of the church.

In conclusion, the church is going to have to make some decisions and take some actions. However, how about some of that change beginning with you — the reader of this book?

Let us now return to the story with which this book was opened. A month has elapsed. Susan did contact the Bishop's office and a joint council meeting of Emmanuel and Zion was called. The Assistant to the Bishop was at the meeting. Bill has now returned home.

"Bill, how did the council meeting go?"

"A lot better than I thought it would. Things don't look so bleak after all."

"What do you mean? Are we going to have a pastor soon?"

"Well, not hardly. Pastor Sharp, that's the name of the Bishop's Assistant, and the name sure fits him, did bring down some names; but when we looked at the proposed budgets it was quite evident that currently we are just not in a position to extend a call to any of them. They were all pastors with several years of experience and rather high in the salary scale. That made things look bleak until he came up with another proposal."

"What kind of other proposal?"

"We have been reading about it once in a while in our church magazine. It is called Indigenous, Bi-Vocational Ministry and Ministry Education by Extension. It sounds kind of far out but we did decide to bring it to a congregational meeting and we voted to recommend its acceptance. The Synod wants to start a pilot project and they thought this part of the country would be a good place to start one since there already are several vacancies around here and some of the larger churches in the towns are looking for some kind of additional staff. Anyway, after we discussed it and thought about it, it began to sound pretty good. You remember, last time when I came home we wondered what Paul would have done in our situation. I believe Paul would have tried something like this. The council came to the same conclusion, so we said, 'Let's go for it. It's an uncharted road but we have little to lose and much to gain.' It's my hope and prayer that the congregation will give it a favorable hearing."

Reflections

As I have been writing this book the thought, "What if?", has often come to my mind. What if the church picks up this proposal and Indigenous, Bi-Vocational Ministry and Ministry Education by Extension actually becomes a reality in many of our congregations? What could result?

Maybe we would see significant growth in our church. Our church planting funds could stretch so much further. We could send a mission developer into a community, and when 10 to 15 households would respond and begin to worship together, the mission developer would give them guidance in the selection and calling of indigenous leadership and get them involved in extension training. The mission developer would then move on. Yes, he or she would keep in contact with them by letter, telephone calls and occasional visits. If problems would develop they would first struggle with them themselves in consultation with the developer or synod staff. When all else fails, then, and only then, would synod intervene.

A group this size would not need to lay out large sums of money for capital development and get involved in large monthly payments. Most communities have a variety of meeting places available. They may not look very "churchly" but that might be an advantage. The unchurched would not have fears about "what lies behind those doors." If they meet in a school, everyone knows what a school looks like. How about public rooms in courthouses, mortuary chapels, doctors' reception rooms, restaurant banquet rooms, open spaces in the mall, rumpus rooms, public parks, theaters and last, but not least, our own living rooms? Many places stand vacant on Sunday mornings. IBVM and MEE would facilitate the church in focusing more on people and less on property. We can envision the multiplication of many new churches. When a congregation would reach a size that would necessitate more space, say 60 to 70 people, the congregation would divide and become two congregations to begin growing again.

We need to envision a host of small congregations that are led and discipled by leadership of their own choosing. Humankind always looks for meaningful relations. The generation that we call "baby boomers," according to some researchers, is especially looking for meaningful relationships. Many, maybe most of them, have moved far away from their childhood ties, have lost the denominational loyalty that their parents had, and are waiting, even seeking, for something to fill the void. What better void filler is there than the Christian gospel, and what better medium is there for the dissemination of that gospel than small congregations, call them "house churches" if you will? I have been blessed by having had the opportunity to serve the church in a variety of situations in Africa, Canada and the United States. In congregations where the average attendance was under 40 persons I have observed that everybody soon got to know everyone else and they had a caring attitude. At the close of the service, as the people were gathering in the back of the church to exchange greetings and personal news, if Sven and Olga were missing, someone would be sure to ask, "Where are Sven and Olga today?" And the question persisted until the answer was known. In other words, Sven and Olga counted! This is one of the qualities that gives these small congregations such tremendous survival power. They can survive even when they are told to close. But one thing they can not survive is the high cost of traditional ministry. When they can no longer "pay the preacher" they are often forced to close. We can envision something better.

All kinds of surveys tell us that an increasing percentage of our population believes that they can be good Christians without belonging to a church. That may or may not be so, but one thing is for certain — the Christian faith will not be passed from one generation to the next without some form of church. It may not be what we have known in the past with beautiful liturgies, accomplished choirs, organs and magnificent buildings. It might be something much simpler. It could just be that the millions and millions of people adrift in our society can be drawn into small group churches pastored and nurtured by ministers of their own group.

Let us pursue the advantages of small group churches further. The September 27, 1989, issue of *The Lutheran* had a news item, "Crumbling City Churches: Museums or Ministries." The Evangelical Lutheran Church in America is faced with large, old city churches that are too costly to maintain, no longer practical for the ministry and too expensive to demolish. The ELCA is not the only church faced with this problem. A drive through the urban areas of any large city will validate it is a common problem. The size of these congregations, congregations that at one time comprised 1,000 to 4,000 members, has diminished so that the few remaining members can no longer support the ministry and building costs. David Opgrand, director for building and services, poses these alternatives, "Should we be preserving the old Gothic structures rather than putting up new buildings for new congregations in growing areas?"[10] The best answer might be "NEITHER."

It may do us well to remember that, when those urban churches were being vacated by people moving to suburbia, new large sanctuaries and educational units were being built in suburban areas. Some of those suburban congregations are now graying and beginning to diminish in size. It could well be that in 30 to 50 years we will be coming up with our second generation of buildings that either need to be repaired or demolished. What a tragic waste of resources! Further, this problem is not limited to the cities. It is also endemic in the countryside. Many rural churches once built for congregations of 300 to 700 members now have very small congregations and are struggling to maintain their ministries and buildings. Are there no possibilities that have brighter prospects than these? Yes, there is an alternative.

First, in the urban areas we must retain ministry. A way to do that is by Indigenous, Bi-Vocational Ministry and Ministry Education by Extension. These small congregations can survive, but not in those huge buildings. For safety's sake the crumbling buildings will have to come down but from the rubble let there arise vibrant congregations which make their own choices of how and where they will worship. Congregations must arise which comprise, at least in part, the ethnic population of the community and are able to reach out to the community. Secondly, let us learn our lesson. Let us desist from building future museum pieces and put our emphasis on people, not property. This might also be a partial solution to the "church shopping" syndrome. Strong attachments to denominations has diminished. Many people no longer seek out a Methodist, Baptist, Lutheran or some other church because of their allegiance to their denomination. They look for the church that has the program they feel they need — strong youth group, Sunday school, music groups, etc. This attitude often leaves the small congregations "out in the cold." They do not have all of these programs. But what these people are really saying is that they need a place where their needs are met. What better place could they be met than in the intimacy of a small congregation where all persons — children, adults, singles, married — would be persons of worth and full participants?

There are human costs which our current model of ministry has that could be alleviated, and in some cases eliminated, by indigenous, bi-vocational ministry. Every pastor who has resigned from one congregation and moved to another understands something of the pain of a move, not only for the pastor, but also for the congregation.

In the pastoral ministry we develop relationships with our people — the children and youth, those in middle years and especially with the elderly. To me the leaving of the elderly has been the most painful. Often you have had the closest contacts with them in their homes and care centers. You remember with intense gratitude the moments you have shared together celebrating the Lord's Supper around a kitchen table. Then it comes time to resign and you must face the question, "How can I explain to them why I am leaving?" Sometimes you even say to yourself, "I would like to be here for this person's funeral." But the ties must be severed and someone, maybe, will step in to take your place and the process begins all over again. Your reasons for leaving — increased salary, being nearer to family — are adequate for you, but do they sometimes sound shallow to those who linger behind?

IBVM could alleviate a lot of this pain. The pastor could very well continue to be a part of the congregation and community even after completion of his/her term of service or retirement. Contact could be maintained. And, development of a cadre of ministers will enhance the concept that the church is always present through a number of persons. Ministry in the Christian church should not be a cause for human pain but rather a way of alleviating human pain.

The stress of career change is another human cost that we need to be aware of and deal with. Previously the crisis of moving from the pastorate into secular employment has been mentioned. Now we need to think about it in the other direction. Increasingly, persons who have had a secular career sense the call to become pastors and enroll in a seminary. This is commendable. However, must they cut off their source of income, get themselves into debt and uproot their families to become pastors? For those who desire to go the full academic route this may be necessary but for many others indigenous, bi-vocational ministry would be a much better option, both for themselves and for the congregations. Our present model of ministry eliminates some candidates for pastoral ministry before they even get started. IBVM and MEE could permit them to maintain a stable life and receive their training and additional part time employment all at the same time. Let us do some serious thinking about this. We can do better! We must do better!

Indigenous, Bi-Vocational Ministry might enable our churches to once again become truly inclusive — embracing men, women, children, youth, aged and people of all ethnic, racial and social backgrounds living in a residential or work area. A casual survey of the New Testament reveals that the apostolic church was inclusive both in membership and leadership. But, today we find it very difficult to cross the barriers we have erected. For too long large segments of society have been excluded, often not intentionally, from full participation in the life of the church. Let us just think of one group — the women.

Since the time of Constantine, maybe earlier, women have been, to a large extent, excluded from pastoral leadership. With the responsibilities of caring and providing for families, just how many women were available to enroll in the traditional seminary? Not very many. But, in the apostolic era and the period briefly following, they were not excluded. Del Birkey, in *The House Church*, points out that in the pre-Constantine era women naturally had positions of leadership equal with men.[11] That happened in a cultural setting that excluded and degraded women. IBVM and MEE can possibly open the doors to many for service in the church because it would not demand disruption of family life. Other positive contributions of IBVM and MEE are that it could provide additional income and the fulfillment of meeting a need in the church.

With these comments this book comes to a close. May the Church of Jesus Christ be bold in vision, high in resolve and committed to the ministry of Word and Sacrament.

Vernon Swenson, Pastor
Reformation Day, 1990

Acknowledgements

1. Joseph Sittler, *Gravity and Grace*, copyright © 1986 Augsburg Publishing House, by permission of Augsburg Fortress, Minneapolis, Minnesota, p. 52.

2. Roland Allen, *Missionary Methods: St. Paul's or Ours?*, Wm. B. Eerdmans Publishing Co., Grand Rapids, Michigan, first published 1912, reprinted 1983, p. 104-107.

3. G. Everett Arden, *Augustana Heritage*, Augustana Press, Rock Island, Illinois, p. 24-25.

4. Sittler, *Gravity and Grace*, p. 53.

5. "Toward A Report On The Ministry," Division for Professional Leadership, Lutheran Church in America, Philadelphia, Pennsylvania, p. 15-16.

6. Allen, *Missionary Methods: St. Paul's or Ours?*, p. 105.

7. John D. Sutherland, "Models of Pastoral Training," in *Lutheran Partners*, March-April, 1988, p. 10.

8. Ingvar Haddal, *John Wesley*, The Epworth Press, London, 1961, p. 105.

9. Allen, *Missionary Methods: St. Paul's or Ours?*, p. 123.

10. "The Lutheran," Evangelical Lutheran Church in America, Chicago, Illinois, September 27, 1989, p. 35.

11. Del Birkey, *The House Church*, Herald Press, Scottsdale, Pennsylvania, 1988, p. 60.

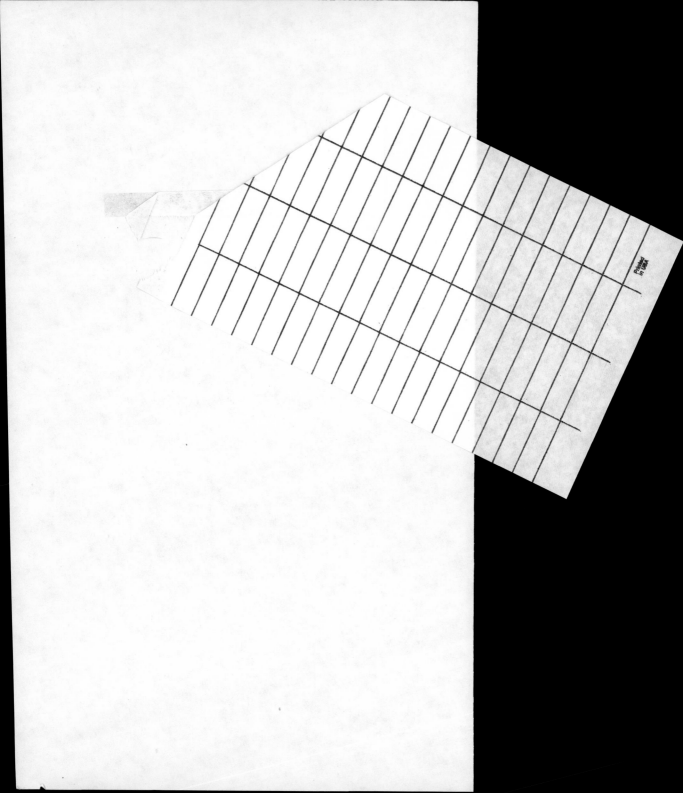